In Pursuit of the Greatest Gift

What the Love Chapter Reveals About Godly Living!

John R. Strubhar

sermontobook
.com

Sermon To Book
www.sermontobook.com

In Pursuit of the Greatest Gift / John R. Strubhar
ISBN-13: 978-1-945793-28-8
ISBN-10: 1-945793-28-7

Dedicated in memory of my father, Dr. Robert C. Strubhar, my mentor and my friend, whose passion for Jesus and the Scriptures continues to motivate and inspire me.

CONTENTS

CONTENTS

Note from the Author

Welcome to *In Pursuit of the Greatest Gift: What the Love Chapter Reveals About Godly Living*!

As you read, you'll find that a workbook section, including questions and application-oriented "action steps," follows each main chapter of the book. The purpose of these action steps is to facilitate reflection on the key characteristics of Christ-like love and how to apply this greatest gift of God in your life.

The workbook sections can be used for independent reflection, discussion with a friend, or group study. You can use the spaces and notes pages provided to write down your responses and other thoughts.

No matter your reason for picking up this book, my prayer is that it will deepen your understanding of "the love chapter" (1 Corinthians 13) and help you begin practicing a more love-based relationship with God and with others. Amen!

—*John R. Strubhar*

INTRODUCTION

Agape Love

And I will show you a still more excellent way. — **1 Corinthians 12:31**

We love our spouse and our children.

We love our parents.

We love God.

We love our country.

We love puppies, cheesecake, cheeseburgers, the color blue, and our favorite movie actor or actress.

'Love' is a word that we use quite often but seldom with complete understanding or intentionality. We may use it reflexively or flippantly, but rarely with consciousness of its proper meaning and full weight.

In other words, we employ this word 'love' frequently, in various ways, and often carelessly. Such is the English language, but when it comes to 'love,' we should take special care, especially as Christ-followers.

Why? Because Christ-followers, of all people, should know that love is all that matters. The Bible tells us so, and Jesus showed us how.

Moreover, this is no ephemeral, cheesy, pop-song love, either. There is absolutely nothing in the world like godly love—the love God has for every single one of us. It gives of itself continually.

Jesus calls us to the same kind of love. When we are truly in love with Him, it changes everything about us—our perspectives, our priorities, and our behavior. It changes the way we relate to Him and to each other. No dimension of our life escapes biblical love because it originates with God, and no one can hide from Him.

Love is the greatest of the gifts God has given us, and ultimately, it's all that matters. All that remains is for us to accept His gift and let it transform us.

Of course, that's easier said than done. In the course of this book, we will discover what godly love is and what it isn't. Let's begin with the word 'love' itself.

The Language of Love

The Greek language of the New Testament is much more descriptive than our modern English language in referring to love. Our English word 'love' is used to describe romance, affection, compassion, and even our relationship to God. Because 'love' is so inclusive in our English language, we fail to understand its precise meaning in specific contexts. By contrast, the Greek language uses three unique words to describe particular forms of this word 'love.'

For romantic or physical love, as between a man and a woman, the Greeks used the word *eros*. This kind of love has its proper place, but the love it denotes is essentially self-gratifying in nature. *Eros* is a matter of fulfilling certain physical and emotional needs through intimate, ultimately physical relationships. *Eros* love is selfishly motivated and gradually became tinged with the idea of lust, eroticism, and pornography. It is the Hollywood kind of love that we never find in the New Testament.

By contrast, *philia* is the Greek word for love rooted in friendship. It is the sort of love that exists between close friends or between parents and their children. *Philia* expresses emotional warmth, fondness, and affection. It is from this root word that we get our English word 'philanthropy.' In John 15:14–15, Jesus calls His disciples "*friends*":

> *You are my friends if you do what I command you. No longer do I call you servants, for the servant does not know what his master is doing; but I have called you friends, for all that I have heard from my Father I have made known to you.* — **John 15:14–15**

The third and highest of all form of love is what the Greeks called *agape*. This love, which takes the form of self-sacrifice and self-giving, is fundamentally other-centered. Thus, when we read John 3:16, we are reading a description of God's *agape* for humanity:

For God so loved the world, that he gave his only Son, that whoever believes in him should not perish but have eternal life. — **John 3:16**

This kind of love is not just warm, gushy, emotional feelings. It is a commitment of the will. God didn't sit up in heaven and have nice, warm feelings for His people. He acted upon His love. He sent Jesus Christ into the world to be our Savior and Lord.

Because it is sacrificial and not self-serving, *agape* love never accepts anything in return. It cannot be compensated, just as we can never compensate God for the gift of His Son in place of our sins. Moreover, *agape* never stops. There is no limit, as God's love never ceases.

While *agape* love cannot be compensated, it can be demonstrated by a changed life in Jesus Christ and a growing relationship to Him through the Word. We will never be able to display this kind of love if we are asleep at the switch. If we are not walking with Him, *agape* love will pass us by.

When *agape* love gets hold of us, it supplies us with a whole new dimension of living. God's gift of *agape* love brings us to the point of decision, and when we receive Jesus, God's *agape* love is *"poured into our hearts through the Holy Spirit who has been given to us"* (Romans 5:5).

The moment we receive Jesus, we receive the Holy Spirit. He comes in and takes over. He removes the self-centered rottenness and junk and fills the resulting void with God's love. Thus, we read:

We love because he first loved us. — *1 John 4:19*

God's *agape* love is ever present with us because of His demonstrated sacrifice for us. In return, we as His disciples are not only to love Him back with a deep, reverent love, but also demonstrate *agape* to other people:

> Love one another: just as I have loved you, you also are to love one another. By this all people will know that you are my disciples, if you have love for one another. — *John 13:34–35*

Agape is all about relationship. As the undeserving recipients of God's incomparable *agape* love, we possess a tremendous capacity to love one another in our relationships—and He expects us to make use of it! As W.E. Vine explains, love is "the characteristic word of Christianity."[1]

Moreover, because God fills us with His other-centered, self-sacrificing love, His Holy Spirit who dwells within us equips us with spiritual gifts to do God's ministry God's way. Indeed, God's purpose for us is that we discover, develop, and deploy these gifts for His glory.

Indeed, God wants His great gift of love to transform us into a people of action who are full of compassion and grace.

Spiritual Gifts

Now concerning spiritual gifts, brothers, I do not want you to be uninformed. You know that when you were pagans you were led astray to mute idols, however you were led. Therefore I want you to understand that no one speaking in the Spirit of God ever says "Jesus is accursed!" and no one can say "Jesus is Lord" except in the Holy Spirit. — 1 Corinthians 12:1–3

Few if any places in the Bible speak more directly or at greater length about *agape* love than does the love chapter—that is, chapter 13 of Paul's First Epistle to the Corinthians. However, to understand the love chapter fully, we must first understand its immediate scriptural context in 1 Corinthians 12–14.

In these chapters, we discover that spiritual gifts are capacities God gives us to serve Him and build up the body of Christ. However, in these chapters, the church in Corinth fails to maintain a right attitude about these God-given gifts.

Spiritual gifts are not given to Christ-followers so they can feel special or spiritually superior to other Christ-followers. Spiritual gifts are intended to be instruments of spiritual effectiveness, not avenues for schism and divisiveness. Paul's desire in these chapters is that the Corinthians stop fighting among themselves and understand the true nature of spiritual gifts.

In 1 Corinthians 12, Paul makes three key observations.

First, all Christ-followers possess the Holy Spirit.
We cannot be a born-from-above Christ-follower and not
have the Holy Spirit in our life:

> *No one speaking in the Spirit of God ever says "Jesus is ac-*
> *cursed!" and no one can say "Jesus is Lord" except in the*
> *Holy Spirit.* — *1 Corinthians 12:3*

The gospel of Jesus Christ and the gift of His Holy
Spirit has transformed the lives of the Corinthian Christians. However, a problem develops when the
Corinthians begin to place special emphasis on the so-
called "miraculous gifts," including speaking in tongues,
miracles, healings. As the Corinthian church elevates
these particular gifts over the fruit of the Holy Spirit, di-
visions begin to arise within the body of Christ.

Thus, in 1 Corinthians 12, we find Paul the apostle
proactively seeking to get the Corinthians believers back
on track. The first fact that Paul needs to establish is that
every single Christ-follower possesses the Holy Spirit. In
other words, the Spirit of God is alive within every
Christ-follower, throwing up red flags whenever we start
to stray off the path Jesus and Scripture have established.

It's the Holy Spirit who constantly maintains and
monitors the *agape* relationship between us and God,
and between us and others.

**Second, all spiritual gifts are the prerogative of
God and not of man.** In the passage below, Paul makes

it clear that God, through the Holy Spirit, is the only One responsible for the spiritual gifts we receive:

> *Now there are varieties of gifts, but the same Spirit; and there are varieties of service, but the same Lord; and there are varieties of activities, but it is the same God who empowers them all in everyone. To each is given the manifestation of the Spirit for the common good. For to one is given through the Spirit the utterance of wisdom, and to another the utterance of knowledge according to the same Spirit, to another faith by the same Spirit, to another gifts of healing by the one Spirit, to another the working of miracles, to another prophecy, to another the ability to distinguish between spirits, to another various kinds of tongues, to another the interpretation of tongues. All these are empowered by one and the same Spirit, who apportions to each one individually as he wills. — 1 Corinthians 12:4–11*

Clearly, when it comes to spiritual gifts, we don't have any decision in the matter other than the choice to accept or reject the gift. We cannot simply manufacture or teach ourselves gifts from above, such as prophesying, healing, miracle-working, and uncommon faith. They are the prerogative of the living God, not ours!

Worth noting is Paul's assertion that no Christ-follower is without one of these gifts by which to minister to others: "*To each is given the manifestation of the Spirit for the common good*" (1 Corinthians 12:7). If we know Jesus Christ and have an *agape*-fueled desire for ministry, then the Holy Spirit gives us the capability. If we have Jesus, then we have the Holy Spirit—and if we have the Spirit, then we have been given spiritual gifts with which to glorify God in ministry for the benefit of others.

And the Spirit, who lives in us, knows us and our respective personalities well enough to know exactly which spiritual gift is best fitted to our personality and temperament:

> *All these are empowered by one and the same Spirit, who apportions to each one individually as he wills.* — **1 Corinthians 12:11**

The Spirit of the God who created us understands our unique spiritual capacities and knows how we can best develop this potential in ways that will honor Him and bring joy to everyone in our lives.

Third, every part of the body of Christ, the church, is equally necessary and important. Paul writes about the parts of the human body—the feet, the hands, the eyes, and the head—to illustrate figuratively the necessity of every member and their role in the body of Christ:

> *For just as the body is one and has many members, and all the members of the body, though many, are one body, so it is with Christ. For in one Spirit we were all baptized into one body—Jews or Greeks, slaves or free—and all were made to drink of one Spirit.*
>
> *For the body does not consist of one member but of many. If the foot should say, "Because I am not a hand, I do not belong to the body," that would not make it any less a part of the body. And if the ear should say, "Because I am*

not an eye, I do not belong to the body," that would not make it any less a part of the body. If the whole body were an eye, where would be the sense of hearing? If the whole body were an ear, where would be the sense of smell? But as it is, God arranged the members in the body, each one of them, as he chose. If all were a single member, where would the body be? As it is, there are many parts, yet one body. **— 1 Corinthians 12:12–20**

Moreover, Paul contends, the most prestigious-seeming members of the body—such as the head, or leadership—are no worthier of honor than the other members:

The eye cannot say to the hand, "I have no need of you," nor again the head to the feet, "I have no need of you." On the contrary, the parts of the body that seem to be weaker are indispensable, and on those parts of the body that we think less honorable we bestow the greater honor, and our unpresentable parts are treated with greater modesty, which our more presentable parts do not require. **— 1 Corinthians 12:21–24**

All members of the body of Christ are also interdependent in their specialized roles, as the parts of the body depend on each other and function (or not) in concert:

But God has so composed the body, giving greater honor to the part that lacked it, that there may be no division in the body, but that the members may have the same care for one another. If one member suffers, all suffer together; if one member is honored, all rejoice together. **— 1 Corinthians 12:24–26**

Every follower of Christ is thus connected to every other Christ-follower. We can't say, "I am going to serve God in isolation." Nor can we say, "I don't like that member of the church—I'm not going to have anything to do with him." If the person who rubs us the wrong way is an ankle in the body, and we're a foot in the body, we'll be in trouble if we cut that person off!

We are all connected; we all need each other. Though the church comprises many unique individuals, when we come together and let the Holy Spirit work through the various spiritual capacities with which He has gifted us, we will be energized and grow, individually and collectively, in ways beyond anything we can ever imagine.

Paul next identifies some of the spiritual roles for which the Holy Spirit empowers believers:

Now you are the body of Christ and individually members of it. And God has appointed in the church first apostles, second prophets, third teachers, then miracles, then gifts of healing, helping, administrating, and various kinds of tongues. Are all apostles? Are all prophets? Are all teachers? Do all work miracles? Do all possess gifts of healing? Do all speak with tongues? Do all interpret? — **1 Corinthians 12:27–30**

Whether our spiritual gift is praying, teaching, healing, administrating, or anything else, don't just sit on it. Don't be content merely to lean back and soak in the deep truths of the Word. Such behavior contributes to spiritual obesity in the body of Christ!

Members of the body serve. We use our gifts in the spirit of *agape* love and are thus transformed.

After acknowledging these spiritual gifts, however, and simultaneously calling out the Corinthians for trying to establish a hierarchy that favored some gifts over others, Paul is ready to redirect their energies toward the greatest gift of all—*agape* love.

> *But earnestly desire the higher gifts.*
>
> *And I will show you a still more excellent way.* — **1 Corinthians 12:31**

These *"higher gifts"* are no doubt the ones Paul was referring to in 1 Corinthians 12:28 when he said, *"And God has appointed in the church first apostles, second prophets, third teachers, then miracles, gifts of healing, helping, administrating and various kinds of tongues."*

What Paul is communicating to them is not a command, but a fact. The verb tense of the phrase *"earnestly desire"* is not imperative, but rather, indicative. In short, Paul is telling the church at Corinth: "You are earnestly desiring the higher gifts or the greater gifts, but listen up! *I will show you a still more excellent way."*

Paul's desire is that the Corinthian church not become hung up on which spiritual gift has greater value than another spiritual gift. He wants God's people to be in pursuit of *"a still more excellent way"*—the way of Christ-like love.

God doesn't want us taking credit for our gifts or boasting about them. He doesn't want us to elevate ourselves over other Christ-followers on the basis of our gifts. Instead, He wants us to focus on using the gifts we have in pursuit of *agape* love—the greatest spiritual gift of all.

God doesn't want us to be known as people who teach, people who speak in tongues, or people who prophesy, but as people who love. In the words of Dr. George Sweeting:

My life and your life minus God's love equals nothing.[2]

The end of 1 Corinthians 12 therefore brings us directly to the heart of the matter: What is love? How do we practice it?

Paul is prepared now to elaborate on these topics by describing what people and relationships full of *agape* look like. And so we arrive at the love chapter.

CHAPTER ONE

When Love Is Absent

If I speak in the tongues of men and of angels, but have not love, I am a noisy gong or a clanging symbol. And if I have prophetic powers, and understand all mysteries and all knowledge, and if I have all faith, so as to remove mountains, but have not love, I am nothing. If I give away all I have, and if I deliver up my body to be burned, but have not love, I gain nothing. — **1 Corinthians 13:1–3**

Many food recipes include a key ingredient that can make or break the dish in question. Just try whipping up some sugar cookies without the sugar or forgetting the yeast in a loaf of bread. The first person to take a bite will know the difference!

In the love chapter, 1 Corinthians 13, Paul clearly establishes that God's *agape* love is the key ingredient in our relationships with each other and in building the kingdom of God. Thus, he begins his discussion of love by helping the Corinthians understand what happens among the body of Christ when love is left out of the recipe.

No Love, No Gifts

Without love, we cannot exhibit genuine spiritual gifts. When love is not evident in the way we exercise our spiritual gifts, Paul explains to the Corinthian church, those gifts become empty and worthless. In this passage, he uses the examples of speaking in tongues, prophesying, spiritual understanding, and spiritual knowledge.

A Noisy Gong and a Clanging Cymbal

> *If I speak in the tongues of men and of angels, but have not love, I am a noisy gong or a clanging cymbal.* **— 1 Corinthians 13:1**

First, love is greater than any kind of speech. Paul begins by speaking to them about the lessor gift—the gift of tongues—that is causing such a stir in Corinth. Some of the Corinthians are arguing that speaking in tongues is the supreme evidence of being controlled directly by the Spirit. Therefore, they suggest, anyone who does not speak in tongues is somehow less gifted or valuable than those who do. Moreover, as ancient Greeks, the Corinthians were culturally infatuated with great orators and rhetoricians, so they are perhaps disposed to look highly on any speech-oriented spiritual gift, be it ecstatic utterance or pure eloquence.

However, Paul quickly disposes of such notions. In reality, he says, speaking in tongues is pure noise if the speaker lacks *agape* in his or her heart. It's no more effective than a reverberating gong or the clashing metal of cymbals, and before long it grates on the ears.

That's why all of us need to be echoing the words of the Psalmist over and over, especially at times when words seem to be flung about carelessly, even from our own mouths:

> *Let the words of my mouth and the meditation of my heart be acceptable in your sight, O LORD, my rock and my redeemer.* — **Psalm 19:14**

Our words matter. Therefore, when we use our spiritual gifts to communicate with others, it's of utmost importance that our words be filled with love. Otherwise, they're just noise.

Powerless Prophets

> *And if I have prophetic powers ... but have not love, I am nothing.* — **1 Corinthians 13:2**

Second, Paul affirms to the Corinthians that love is greater than the power of prophecy. Prophecy ranks second in Paul's order of the gifts of the Spirit in 1 Corinthians 12:28. The word 'prophet' comes from a Greek word meaning "to cause to shine" and is linked to a prefix meaning "before." A prophet is one who stands before and causes the Word of God to shine—that is, to be amplified and clarified in such a way that people will understand and grasp it. A prophet does not originate anything new, but rather takes the revealed Word of God, causing it to come alive in the hearts of those who are hearing its message.

The prophets of the Old Testament—men such as Elijah, Isaiah, Jeremiah, Ezekiel, Daniel, Jonah, and numerous others—speak God's truth. Prophecy has a connotation of telling the future, and sometimes prophets' words of truth pertain to the future because God exists across time in a way we do not. At other times, these prophets amplify what God has previously revealed in His Word.

Prophets speak or write God's truth while the Holy Spirit attends them so fully that they communicate His words without error. Yet if they had acted without love, even the most gifted of these prophets would have been uncommendable, inadequate, and without impact from an eternal perspective.

In early modern times, God raised up great reformers like Luther, Calvin, and Wesley with the gift of prophecy. These were men who caused the Word of God to come alive in the hearts of those who heard its message.

Today, we read and hear the words of notable pastors and teachers like John MacArthur, Charles Swindoll, Charles and Andy Stanley, David Jeremiah, and others who also help us more fully understand and apply the Scriptures to our lives.

As with the prophets of old, these modern men of God grow our understanding of God's will and purpose. The Word of God opens to them so that their voices speak truth in helping us understand passages of Scripture that would otherwise tend to produce questions, doubt, and false interpretation.

Nonetheless, if such insight, which we may consider prophetic, is not employed in love, it amounts to nothing.

Meaningless Mysteries

> And if I have prophetic powers, and understand all mysteries ... but have not love, I am nothing. — 1 Corinthians 13:2

Third, and closely related to Paul's mention of the spiritual gift of prophecy, is his assertion that love is greater than "*understanding all mysteries.*"

Here Paul refers to the divine insight God gives to those who are diligent students of the Word of God, which may include individuals from the list of reformers and teachers in the previous section on prophetic powers. As each of those modern-day prophets understands well, we cannot grasp the mysteries of God until we are, first of all, students of His Word.

Too many people today want to know the mysteries of God but are not willing to do the hard work of Bible study to arrive at these deep truths. They prefer to take what others say about the Bible and pass it on as something that is true, but they cannot attest to their claims from the personal experience of one-on-one engagement with God's Word.

Perhaps you've experienced for yourself the understanding that comes from intensive Bible study. Maybe you've read a passage repeatedly when, suddenly, a light turns on in your mind and you perceive the connections between two or more different Scripture passages. In that moment, we begin to understand how it all fits together, and as a result we understand a new dimension of God's character. Such revelation comes from a habit of digging deeply into the Word of God.

Unfortunately, many members of the Christian community want other people to do their thinking for them. They may be obsessed with uncovering hidden truths of God, but they don't think they need to put any real, patient effort into the discovery process.

And even more regrettably, some Christ-followers are far more concerned with soaking in spiritual taking in content than practicing it. They don't concern themselves with loving difficult people, even though God loves such people and expects us to do the same. Paul's words in 1 Corinthians 13:2 are clear. If we don't care about developing *agape*-based relationships with others, regardless of our differences or their shortcomings, then we aren't following the way of Jesus Christ and we don't truly understand anything about God's great love.

Moreover, if our relationships with our brothers and sisters in Christ are not characterized by love, then the Scriptures won't make any sense to us. We can read and read, but the Bible will seem disjointed and full of contradictions. It won't make any sense.

But if we approach God and His Word with a heart full of love for Him and for each other, then the Spirit will reveal to us the answers and truths we seek.

Building Up, Not Puffing Up

And if I have prophetic powers, and understand all mysteries and all knowledge ... but have not love, I am nothing. — **1 Corinthians 13:2**

Fourth, as with having prophetic power and understanding spiritual mysteries, for understanding and knowledge to be meaningful in God's eyes, love is required.

If mere knowledge were the key to success, we would be a successful generation, indeed! Thanks in large part to the internet, as well as to continual advancements in science, technology, and other research, knowledge is exploding in our society and culture today. In the midst of this information age, our human nature inclines us to pride ourselves on the particular kinds of knowledge we've amassed.

However, men and women today seem more miserable than ever. They are constantly finding what is wrong with something or someone and searching for fault instead of appreciating what is commendable. As a result, some of the most intelligent people alive who have heads brimming with knowledge are also some of the unhappiest. Humanity collectively knows more than ever before, yet our problems and suffering are in many ways as severe as ever, or worse.

Many Christ-followers are no different when it comes to their pride in amassing biblical knowledge: the better versed Christ-followers become in reciting scriptures, articulating doctrine, and analyzing spiritual principles, the more tempted they are to think themselves superior to those who know less. Meanwhile, they struggle to get along with other people, even within the body of Christ!

It is doubtless the same in ancient times, including in Corinth. Thus, Paul writes earlier in his letter to the Corinthian church:

> *This "knowledge" puffs up, but loves builds up. If anyone imagines that he knows something, he does not yet know as he ought to know.* **— 1 Corinthians 8:1–2**

While *"knowledge' puffs [us] up"* in pride, love builds us up for God's purposes. Paul is not contending that ignorance is preferable to knowledge—which it's not. Rather, Paul wants the Corinthians to bring knowledge together with love. He wants believers not merely to know something but also to love Someone (God) and others, in a perfect blend of knowledge and *agape*.

Over the years, I have had the privilege of working with some of God's choicest servants. My mentor at Trinity Evangelical Divinity School was Dr. Lloyd Perry, a godly man who had earned three doctorates. I never once heard Dr. Perry talk about his academic pedigree. Never once did he strut around campus with the attitude that other people needed to listen to him because of the degrees and knowledge he had acquired. To the contrary, Dr. Perry was probably one of the most humble, gracious men I have ever known. When you were around him, you weren't aware of his academic achievements—you were aware of Jesus.

And the same can be said of Dr. John R. W. Stott. Perhaps I didn't agree with every word he wrote, but he was exceptionally gifted in knowledge. More importantly, however, he was truly a man of God, gracious and kind.

People who are on an academic ego trip are always discussing their degrees, but that doesn't mean a thing when people are dying spiritually by degrees. But when we wed knowledge and love, as Dr. Perry and Dr. Stott did, we possess both a keen mind and a warm heart, which God can use in exciting and powerful ways for His glory.

No Love, No Vision

And if I have all faith, so as to remove mountains, but have not love, I am nothing. If I give away all I have, and if I deliver up my body to be burned, but have not love, I gain nothing. **— 1 Corinthians 13:2**

When love is absent in our Christian communities, not only are our spiritual gifts inadequate, but also our spiritual vision is rendered ineffective. Paul refers to spiritual vision as *"all faith, so as to remove mountains,"* because the gift of faith is the ability to see things from God's point of view, which few can see. Through the Holy Spirit, God gifts some of His children with the capacity to see things that are not apparent to others and to be tomorrow-minded, today. The faith to move mountains is the vision to accomplish something which seems impossible to others.

In Hebrews 11, we find a recounting of some of the great men and women of faith. This biblical Hall of Faith ranges from the leading men of Genesis—including Abraham, Isaac, and Jacob—to later luminaries like Joseph, Moses, Samuel, and David. Also mentioned are Rahab, who helps Joshua's army conquer Jericho, and the Judges who led the Israelites before the days of Saul and David. God equips these heroes and heroines with faith, as He does Noah, who builds a massive ark in preparation for the flood even when his neighbors think him crazy and his goal impossible.

Though not all of these figures receive equal mention in our sermons and Bible studies, they share one thing in common: their faith-infused spiritual vision enables each to achieve remarkable things that they are incapable of doing out of their human energy alone.

God is stirring the gift of faith within many of us now. He wants us to be sensitive to the nudgings and promptings of the Holy Spirit. He wants us to believe that God can accomplish things through us when nobody else believes it is possible. But again, vision not rooted in other-centered, Christ-like love ends up in ruin. To be so far ahead of others that we are intolerant and critical of them is not what God requires. Indeed, without Christ-like love, our spiritual vision will remain near-sighted.

We must use the gifts God gives us wisely remembering we are saved by faith, not by our human efforts. Accordingly, God wants us to act humbly and lovingly toward the people who don't catch up with our vision.

We are to live by faith, exercising our spiritual gift of faith and vision, but always within the context of *agape* love.

No Love, No Sacrifice

If I give away all I have, and if I deliver up my body to be burned, but have not love, I gain nothing. — **1 Corinthians 13:3**

Like spiritual gifts and spiritual vision, meaningful spiritual sacrifice is lacking when love is absent. We can do all kinds of good deeds, but if they're not done in love, we are left with a big goose egg.

Paul tells the Corinthians that love is greater than generosity—hence, "*If I give away all I have....*" This is a remarkable assertion, however, considering the immense potential for good to be accomplished if an extremely wealthy person were to liquidate the entirety of his or her assets. Imagine millions of dollars distributed to people in need. Think of the families that would come off welfare, the students who could receive a college education, or the medical assistance that could be rendered to prevent and cure diseases.

Yet Paul knows that all of the generous giving in the world adds up to nothing if it's not done with love. If a desire for recognition motivates our generosity—if we're looking for good publicity or our name on a plaque, then we have sacrificed for the wrong reasons.

We don't give to be recognized or celebrated. Rather, we give to advance the kingdom of God. We forget about who receives the credit. Yes, we are to give to others until it hurts. However, we can give until we ourselves are poverty-stricken but receive no accolades in heaven if we're not operating out of selfless, *agape* love.

Paul is not done. He continues by saying that *agape* love is greater than martyrdom, or delivering his *"body to be burned."* The phrase *"to be burned"* stands for the worst thing that could ever happen to one's body.

Charles Allen, in his book *The Miracle of Love,* relates that the generation to which Paul writes practiced the slave trade.[3] Just as ranchers today brand cattle, human beings were branded as slaves. When the hot iron was applied to their flesh, they wore that mark the rest of their lives. Paul's point is clear: if we give our bodies to be branded as slaves and yet do not have love, our act of self-sacrifice is of no value.

Sometimes we read on the internet or in the newspaper about people who set themselves on fire for a particular cause or to protest a certain governmental policy. Others engage in hunger strikes and fasts to communicate their messages. In some cases, they even die because of their devotion to what they consider to be a high ideal. But the bottom line is the same—if martyrdom is not done in love, it's all in vain.

Indeed, sometimes we can even play the role of a martyr, which in reality is a form of selfishness. We do it to be appreciated, to get noticed, or to solicit the attention we believe we deserve. But that's not sacrifice; it is selfishness on display!

Because Love Is Greater

What messages should we take away from Paul's assessment of spiritual gifts without love?

1. **Because love is greater than any kind of speech, we should ask God to use our lips to speak messages of love, joy, and hope into others' lives.** Let us ask Him to use our lips to articulate kindness to others instead of issuing criticism and complaints. As the Proverbial writer explains in Proverbs 25:11: *"A word fitly spoken is like apples of gold in a setting of silver."*

2. **Because love is greater than knowledge, we must surrender our mind to the Lord.** Far too many of us let others do our thinking for us. Instead, let the love of Jesus govern our thoughts and decisions.

3. **Because love is greater than mountain-moving faith and vision, we should ask God to help us dream big dreams.** From a human standpoint, a dream might seem impossible, but no dream is too big for God. We must ensure, however, that our dream is fueled by His love.

4. **Because love is greater than any act of kindness or self-sacrifice, let us invest our time and resources in things that pay eternal dividends.** Our love for God and, by extension, for other people ought to be our consuming passion in life. Therefore, we must be willing to surrender any and all of our earthly possessions lovingly for the good of others, as He directs us.

There is much for us to learn and experience in the practice of the spiritual gifts with which God has blessed us. But the first and most important imperative is to surrender our gifts back to God so that we always exercise them with His love in our hearts. And as we do, may each of us fall more deeply in love with Him.

WORKBOOK

Chapter 1 Questions

Question: With what spiritual gift has the Holy Spirit blessed you? How do you use this gift? How does your use of your gift glorify God?

_____

_____

_____

_____

_____

_____

_____

_____

_____

_____

_____

_____

Question: How can you use your spiritual gifts in ways that better communicate God's *agape* love to others?

_____

_____

_____

_____

_____

_____

_____

_____

_____

_____

Question: What kind of routine do you have, or could you develop, to spend time with God and immerse yourself in His Word? What obstacles or hang-ups prevent you from spending more concentrated alone time with God, and how can you overcome or address those hindrances?

_____

_____

_____

_____

_____

_____

_____

_____

_____

_____

Action: Thank God for all of the amazing gifts He gives you! Embrace whatever spiritual gift He has specially chosen for you. Use your lips to speak messages of hope and truth, and make a habit of digging deeply in His Word to uncover its mysteries. Dream big for God! But in everything you speak, write, study, dream, and do, surrender your mind to the Lord so that you are thinking God's thoughts. Moreover, let His love fill and flow from your heart to others. Remember, if you aren't loving, nothing else matters. Therefore, filled with *agape*, let God direct your gifts and use you in ways you never imagined!

Chapter 1 Notes

_____

_____

_____

_____

_____

_____

_____

_____

_____

_____

_____

_____

_____

_____

_____

_____

_____

_____

_____

_____

_____

CHAPTER TWO

How Love Acts

Love is patient and kind; love does not envy or boast; it is not arrogant or rude. It does not insist on its own way; it is not irritable or resentful. — **1 Corinthians 13:4–5**

'Love' is more than a word. It is action, in motion.

Once, a pastor friend of mine noticed a notebook left behind at the school bus stop in front of his house. He went outside and picked it up, intending to take it to the school.

As he took a quick glance inside the notebook, however, he noticed that while various kinds of lecture notes filled the pages, the margins were full of doodles. Prominent among the scribblings in the margins was the message "CS + KC = Forever."

Similar doodles continued for several pages of the notebook, but then the pastor noticed a page in which 'Forever' had been scratched out. In its place, the student had written, "Forget it."

Alas, such is the way of young love. It's on again, off again—it doesn't last.

By contrast, the love of God goes beyond anything we will ever know or experience in this life. It is a supernatural kind of love, which by faith we receive into our lives:

> God's love has been poured into our hearts through the Holy Spirit who has been given to us. — **Romans 5:5**

Through God's *agape* love, He transforms our nature. First Corinthians 13, the love chapter, is all about the changes that happen to us when, by faith, we put our trust in the Lord Jesus Christ. Paul illustrates for the Corinthian church how God's love remakes and remolds believers into men and women who live supernaturally in the power of the Holy Spirit.

However, Paul wants the Corinthians to understand that we must also invest *agape* love in our relationships with God and with other people. When we are in love with another person, we forget about ourselves and focus our attention on the one whose love we value. We want to spend more than we can afford and promise more than we can deliver. Falling in love and being in love helps to make life seem worthwhile, but for love to remain strong, it must be cultivated and controlled by a dynamic sense of commitment and trust.

This is true not only in the realm of marital love, between husband and a wife, but also in the spiritual realm. As we receive *agape* love from God when we place our faith in Christ, we must also nurture His love. Christ-like love is transparently unselfish. It does not blow its own horn. It is not on the lookout for its own interests.

When we take God's love for granted, our lives begin to unravel. The most important thing we can do to cultivate the love He pours into us is to obey His Word. That is, we must demonstrate Christ-like love through active obedience to His will:

> *And by this we know that we have come to know him, if we keep his commandments. Whoever says "I know him" but does not keep his commandments is a liar, and the truth is not in him, but whoever keeps his word, in him truly the love of God is perfected. By this we may know that we are in him: whoever says he abides in him ought to walk in the same way in which he walked.* **— 1 John 2:3-6**

These words are powerful! God calls us, as Christ-followers, to walk as Jesus walked, not necessarily as others in the Christian community walk. Paul calls this way of living a *"still more excellent way"* (1 Corinthians 12:31). Christ-like love is the greatest of all loves. When it is absent, our spiritual gifts are inadequate, our spiritual vision is ineffective, and our spiritual sacrifice is insufficient.

Moreover, to keep His Word, we must know it. Sometimes we know a scripture so well that we overlook its true meaning. We read without even realizing we don't fully understand. But if keeping God's Word is key to practicing *agape* love, and *agape* is key to meaningful relationships with God and with other people, then understanding every single word of Scripture becomes crucial.

Paul is graphic as he examines Christ-like love's code of conduct, word by word. As we will soon discover, love's action code is distinctively different and refreshingly real!

Patient During Trials

*Love is patient... — **1 Corinthians 13:4***

When the description of love in 1 Corinthians 13:4–7 is read at weddings, couples tend to get stars in their eyes, while the attendees smile at Paul's sweet-sounding words. Most people don't give a moment's serious thought to the enormous depth of commitment these words require of the bride and groom. This passage is a statement of God's loving action code that sums up the *"more excellent way"* to which Paul refers in 1 Corinthians 12:31.

Significantly, every action and disposition described in this passage occurs in the present tense, which indicates they are supposed to be ongoing—that is, they are meant to be habitual ways of living. God calls all Christ-followers to embrace this way.

God's call to His *"more excellent way"* sounds appealing, but practicing it is a challenge. However, with God's help, we can do so. And Jesus provides us a living, walking example of this way of love. Wherever Jesus walks, He demonstrates the qualities and attitudes found in 1 Corinthians 13:4–7. Therefore, He calls us to live out this list of love, emulating Him, as we follow Him with our whole heart.

The love list begins with **patience**, which blends together the concepts of endurance and longsuffering. The focus here is on our relationships with people, rather than dealing with the circumstances or actions that cross our paths in the processes of life. *Agape* love, in short, takes a long time to boil over.

Remember how patient Jesus is with His disciples: repeatedly, He teaches them truth, but they fumble the ball over and over again and miss the significance of what He says. But does Jesus get annoyed or blow up at them? Does He write them off? No, He continues to reiterate principles of the Kingdom.

Like Jesus, we too, are not to respond in anger. We are called to be patient with one another, even in the hour of our greatest trial. Isn't Jesus patient and longsuffering throughout the agony of His crucifixion? He patiently endures to the very end as He obediently takes upon Himself the sins of humankind.

Because of the patience of Jesus' love for God and for us, under the most extreme circumstances, He receives eternal glory and honor:

God has exalted him and bestowed on him the name that is above every name... — **Philippians 2:9**

Jesus' example ought to stimulate us to endure patiently in our family relationships, our church relationships, and our work relationships. God expects us to stop responding to people and situations the way our human natures incline us to respond. Instead of taking matters into our own hands or making snap judgments about others, we must learn to allow the Holy Spirit to respond for us in *love*.

The Kindness That Binds

Love is patient and kind... — 1 Corinthians 13:4

Patience, despite the strength and persistence it requires, has connotations of passivity because it reflects the immovable side of love. By contrast, **kindness** reflects the more active side of love. It indicates the demonstration of deep affection and implies a slowness to take offense, which makes us easy to get along with.

There is no room in *agape* love for us to carry a chip on our shoulder. Rather, we must treat other people with the same consideration we would our friends or relatives.

Goethe, the German poet, explains kindness as "the golden chain by which society is bound together."[4] People respond well to kindness, which makes it especially vital in marital relationships. What a woman needs from her husband more than anything else is kindness, even when his mind is focused on providing for the family, and a man needs kindness from his wife, even when he falls short of her expectations. As a pastor, I've found myself amazed at how some married women, with financial security and children they love, are willing to give it all up just because someone besides their husband shows them kindness.

While crucial for marriage, kindness is also desperately needed in our churches, neighborhoods, and halls of government. God knows what He is doing when He calls us to a life of kindness. When our patience wears thin with the limitations of others, we can shore it up with acts of kindness.

One of the most difficult things God calls us to do is be kind toward others who are not kind toward us. This requires a supernatural kind of love, indeed! With God, however, such kindness is possible for us. Stephen, the first martyr of the church, seeks God in prayer when facing death by stoning because of his faith in Christ: *"Lord, do not hold this sin against them,"* he prays as they execute him (Acts 7:60). Instead of expressing bitterness, he demonstrates undiluted kindness in using his dying breath to ask God for mercy on behalf of his enemies.

Accordingly, Paul exhorts the Ephesians:

> *Be kind to one another, tenderhearted, forgiving one another, as God in Christ forgave you.* — **Ephesians 4:32**

Though frequently underrated, kindness is a powerful and vibrant expression of love. Godly kindness is always ready to forgive and move on, compelled by the bonds of Christ's love. Interestingly, one of the root ideas of the original word for 'kindness' is 'usefulness.' When we are kind, we are useful to our Lord. But the reverse is also true: when we are unkind, our usefulness for the Kingdom is short-circuited and undermined.

Nailing Envy to the Cross

...love does not envy... — *1 Corinthians 13:4*

However, when we are unkind to each other, we are depriving ourselves and God of opportunities to love and bless other people. Our preoccupation with each other's flaws, and other unkind attitudes, undermines our kingdom-building potential, shatters our witness for Christ, and deprives us of joy.

One of the primary forms of unkindness is **envy**. When we're discontent because someone else has something we want but can't have, that simmering desire can eventually become a boiling anger and turn into envy. This combination of anger and selfish desire is a form of hatred that has no place in the hearts of those controlled by a*gape* love. Moreover, envy is self-destructive, as Solomon observes:

A tranquil heart gives life to the flesh, but envy makes the bones rot. — *Proverbs 14:30*

Discontent with the good fortune of others—whether in terms of their clothing, their car, their job, their position in their home, or any other respect—can thus lead to misery. And in its worst forms, envy can lead us to intentionally making others as miserable as we are, for instance, by gossiping and lying to destroy the other person's reputation. Envy is less concerned with acquiring the object of our desires and more preoccupied with lowering others to our own state of discontent. The ensuing gossip, resentment, and bitterness can spread throughout a whole community if left unchecked.

In that sense, envy is like a disease—a dreadful disease that destroys relationships, breaks homes, and divides churches. Envy of God's supreme position and the worship He received is what prompted Satan to try to dethrone Him, which led God to kick him out of heaven in the first place. Think of the collateral damage Satan's envy has inflicted on humankind ever since!

According to the Scriptures, envy is a sign of worldliness, carnality, and spiritual immaturity. Earlier in his first letter to the Corinthians, Paul writes:

> *For you are still of the flesh. For a while there is jealously and strife among you, are you not of the flesh and behaving only in a human way?* — **1 Corinthians 3:3**

If we are envious of each other's possessions and jealous of each other's relationships, then we are "*still of the flesh*" and "*behaving only in a human way,*" not in the "*more excellent way*" that Jesus shows us and Paul prescribes. Thus, envy prevents our new nature in Christ from supplanting our old nature. Instead of being kind and considerate toward one another, we seek only to manipulate and destroy each other when envy controls us.

Thankfully, when we place Jesus Christ on the throne of our life, He casts out envy from our hearts. His love is the antidote to envy. Love prevents us from gloating over others' failings and misfortunes, instead of enabling us to rejoice in their successes. When others excel past us, Christ-like love empowers us to encourage and support their efforts.

God doesn't want our old nature, including envy, to control us because it is incompatible with our new nature. Therefore, we must crucify envy every day by nailing it to the cross of Christ with kindness.

Boasting Only in the Cross

...love does not envy or boast... — 1 Corinthians 13:4

Have you ever been in conversation with someone who goes on and on about what a tremendous person he or she is, or about all of their accomplishments and successes, without ever pausing to ask what's going on in your life? Or have you ever caught yourself repeatedly redirecting conversation in ways that build yourself up?

That's what Paul means when he warns that love doesn't **boast**: when God's love fills our heart, we won't engage in personal advancement campaigns or any other excessive and flattering speech about ourselves. We won't show off or seek the spotlight. In the prime of his boxing career, Muhammad Ali boasted that he was "the greatest" and sought to brand himself that way. He let everyone know he was the best thing ever to happen to boxing.

The sad thing is that some Christ-followers have fallen into the same trap. They let their egos get the best of them because God has blessed their ministries and accomplished things for or through them that go far beyond their wildest imaginations. Instead of giving the glory back to God, alas, they tend to speak as if God wouldn't have had a chance in accomplishing such feats without their help. They delude themselves into thinking they're indispensable to God's plans.

How tragic! Egotism at its core is edging God out of our lives. This kind of boasting does not advance the gospel. When our ego takes over in this way, it pushes God to the sidelines. However, instead of letting our ego edge God out of our lives, we should be redirecting the focus back to Him.

Christ-followers pursuing the *"more excellent way"* of love do not glory in their personal accomplishments. They never call attention to what they have done, but they call attention to Jesus and to Him alone without whom none of their accomplishments would ever have come to pass. True Christ-followers nurture humility, not self-aggrandizement.

Hence, Paul writes to the Galatians:

But far be it for me to boast except in the cross of our Lord Jesus Christ, by which the world has been crucified to me, and I to the world. — **Galatians 6:14**

The only time we should boast is when we're boasting about Jesus—about what He accomplished on the cross and continues to accomplish in our lives. We are the ones who should be standing on the sidelines, cheering on King Jesus!

Big-Hearted, Not Big-Headed

*...it [love] is not arrogant... — **1 Corinthians 13:4***

Boastfulness often leads to **arrogance**, or an inflated ego and a swollen sense of one's own worth. When we display arrogance, we are missing the fact that God has called each one of us to surrender to Him.

Unchecked, arrogance becomes a habitual attitude of spiritual pride. We suffer delusions of our own, believing ourselves to have reached heights of success or status beyond what other people have achieved.

Therefore, beware of any person who conveys to you that he or she is better than you are. Such arrogance is not of Christ:

> *Everyone who is arrogant in heart is an abomination to the LORD; be assured, he will not go unpunished. — **Proverbs 16:5***

As Christ-followers, we should avoid at all costs becoming "*an abomination to the LORD*"! Arrogance does not please Him in the least, and be assured, it will not go without consequences.

Spiritual arrogance, or feelings of superiority to other Christ-followers is a special concern for those of us in the body of Christ. Simply because we have had a certain experience with God, we may be tempted to feel our spiritual reality has been validated to a greater degree than is true for others.

Spiritual arrogance is the sin that the Pharisees exhibit in their dealings with Jesus. Hence, Jesus chastises the Pharisee who, *"standing by himself, prayed thus: God, I thank you that I am not like other men, extortioners, unjust, adulterers, or even like this tax collector"* (Luke 18:11). Jesus doesn't treat others as inferior to Himself, and God expects us to follow His example.

Thus, James writes, God acts to aid the humble in opposition to those who display spiritual pride or arrogance:

> *But he gives more grace. Therefore it says, "God opposes the proud but gives grace to the humble." — James 4:6*

Pride, or a smug spiritual reality, is offensive to God because apart from Him, none of us are capable of getting our act together or accomplishing anything of eternal significance. All of us make mistakes—and if you think otherwise, just ask your spouse or a close family member to set you straight!

None of us have arrived. None of us have reached a place of perfection. Rather, we are all people on a journey, and only God's love, freely given and not earned by our meager deeds, can get us to the destination.

In short, arrogance is a dead-end street. This includes not only spiritual arrogance but also intellectual, social, and material arrogance. Intellectual arrogance looks down upon the unlearned or those with fewer academic degrees, perhaps considering such people unworthy of conversation. Social arrogance is the sense that we're somehow superior because of our privileged environment or greater exposure to high culture. Material arrogance, meanwhile, is thinking we are better than people who have fewer or inferior possessions, or whose income is less than ours.

But God doesn't care how many degrees we have, how many operas and art shows we've seen, how big our house is, or how much money is in our bank accounts. Scripture is unequivocal on this front:

> *Live in harmony with one another. Do not be haughty, but associate with the lowly. Never be wise in your own sight.*
> *— Romans 12:16*

With every type of arrogance and the haughty attitude it produces, we forget that God is the giver of *"every good and perfect gift"* (James 1:17). That is, everything we possess (that is worth possessing) has been given to us by God as an expression of His love and grace. We haven't earned His blessings of faith, intelligence, knowledge, social status, wealth, or any other variety. Rather, God chooses us to be good stewards of His bounty. When arrogance gets the best of us, however, that bounty becomes a cancer that eats away at our spiritual life.

Thus, arrogance is deadly, but those who travel the more excellent path of love don't fall into its trap. Love is big-hearted toward others, not big-headed. It focuses on Jesus, and on other people for His sake, not on ourselves. *Agape* love never says, in any way, "I'm better than you."

John the Baptist, the forerunner of Jesus Christ, provides us an excellent example of loving humility before God when he declares, "He [Christ] must increase, but I must decrease" (John 3:30). That's what God expects from us as His children: to advance His agenda in place of ours, for the glory of the King of kings and Lord of lords.

Consistently Christ-like

Love ... is not arrogant or rude. — *1 Corinthians 13:4–5*

All we need to do is check the latest headlines or watch a cable news show to see that courtesy is in short supply in many quarters of our society nowadays. Yet as Christ-followers, we live under an imperative to be polite, even when we disagree and even in arenas where rudeness has become the norm.

Though Jesus' words are shocking at times—such as when He says, *"Truly, truly, I say to you, before Abraham was, I am"* (John 8:58)—He is never rude. In fact, nothing turns off non-Christians more quickly and decisively than inconsistency between the *agape* love we profess to live by and our rude behavior toward others.

When a passing car cuts us off without signaling or nearly runs us off the road, we should never see a "Honk If You Love Jesus" sticker plastered to their bumper. And our reaction shouldn't involve slamming on the accelerator and trying to run them into a ditch, either.

Such hypocrisy hurts the body of Christ, undermines the advancement of the kingdom, and offends God. Thus, consistency in our treatment of others is not an option, but a requirement of love.

For this reason, Paul informs the Corinthians that love is not **rude** or obnoxious—it's unfailingly polite. Some people may contend that courtesy in the small matters of life is trivial, but our politeness is a testimony to our love for one another.

Politeness is as simple as saying "thank you" to help create an environment in which others feel loved and appreciated. It also means that we are to be tactful and avoid giving offense if there's any other option.

In his letter to the Philippians, Paul describes the attitude of humility and selflessness that prevents and counteracts rudeness:

> *Do nothing from selfish ambition or conceit, but in humility count others more significant than yourselves.*
> *— Philippians 2:3*

If all of us would practice the simple principle of regarding others as more important than ourselves, our churches, homes, and businesses would be transformed.

Though foreign to our culture today, other-centeredness lies at the heart of divine love.

Today we live in an "every man for himself" world. Like young children declaring, "This is my doll!" or "That's my truck!" we decide that if others don't play nice with us, we won't play with them nicely, either, or at all. Our adult version of this attitude might involve ignoring another person, blocking his or her calls, or "unfriending" him or her on our social media accounts. Rather than try to win the other person over with kindness, we indignantly turn and go a different way.

How completely different is God's love as revealed in Christ:

> But emptied himself, by taking the form of a servant, being born in the likeness of men. And being found in human form, he humbled himself by becoming obedient to the point of death, even death on a cross. — **Philippians 2:7–8**

Our Lord Jesus, while He was here on earth, had a North Star to guide Him: the will of His Father. Unfortunately, far too many of us, even those of us in the body of Christ, live each day without any discernible guide. We choose to do our own thing, and therefore our old human nature controls us—the nature that we supposedly crucified with the blood of Christ. As a result, our human nature constantly interrupts what God wants to accomplish in our lives.

When Christ's spirit of humility grabs hold of us, however, and becomes the guiding force in our relationship with others, then we become less critical, harsh, and rude with one another. This is when God accomplishes His purposes through us. When His love is real, we won't have to go around saying we love one another, because our love will be evident in our every word and action. As we serve one another humbly, giving credit only to God, our *agape* love will speak for itself.

Other-Minded Love

It [love] does not insist on its own way... — **1 Corinthians 13:5**

Christ-like love, then, is not selfish. Because it's not proud, arrogant, or boastful, *agape* doesn't push itself into the limelight. It doesn't compel us to strive for a better position. Selfishness isn't merely an isolated behavior. It's a way of life that runs contrary to God's *"more excellent way"*—because ultimately, it excludes God.

In Paul's second letter to Timothy, he describes the generation just before the Lord returns to be a society in love with itself. Before Christ arrives, people will love themselves and their wealth, without regard for others or for God:

But understand this, that in the last days there will come times of difficulty. For people will be lovers of self, lovers of money, proud, arrogant, abusive, disobedient to their parents, ungrateful, unholy... — **2 Timothy 3:1–2**

Paul's exposition of godly love to the Corinthians runs entirely counter to his description of the *"times of difficulty."* Instead of modeling ourselves after the culture around us, we are to be Christ-controlled and others-minded. We are to focus on everything God has done for us, and we are to offer Him praise and thanksgiving. We are to be generous with the spiritual gifts and resources with which He has blessed us. Instead of being *"lovers of self, lovers of money,"* we are to be people who share and give of ourselves continually.

The gospel message of Christ tells us to forget about ourselves and concentrate on Him. Only when we exchange our preoccupation with ourselves for God's love can we truly be happy, productive, and blessed in all of our relationships.

Once I served in a large church in California that had a staff of about a dozen pastors. The general staff numbered close to fifty people at the time. And when I first arrived at the church, everyone was guarding their own turf. No one shared ministries or cared what was going on in a different sphere of the church's operations.

So preoccupied were the staff members with doing their own thing, the atmosphere of love and harmony that should have existed was giving way to an environment of competition and arrogance.

By the grace of God, however, the staff began to understand that they could accomplish so much more for the church and for the kingdom if they worked together instead of in isolation. God broke down the walls that the staff had erected out of a desire for self-advancement, including the barriers in their own hearts, and they began to glorify God for each other's successes. Hearts melted and came together.

This is what God's other-minded love alone can accomplish!

No Touchiness or Temper

...it [love] is not irritable... — 1 Corinthians 13:5

When Paul writes that love is not **irritable**, he means that love is not provoked. Christ-like love does not give in to exasperation or the letting off steam when we find ourselves in a difficult circumstance or dealing with a difficult person.

No, Paul doesn't write that it is okay to be provoked only occasionally or briefly. Godly love never loses its cool. It never becomes ticked or bitter or uncharitable in thought or word. We in the body of Christ must stop thinking it's okay to react to others out of our feelings of irritation!

Interestingly, the only other time this verb '*irritate*' or '*provoke*' occurs in the New Testament is in the book of Acts:

Now while Paul was waiting for them at Athens, his spirit was provoked within him as he saw that the city was full of idols. — Acts 17:16

What provokes Paul is not the people of Athens, but rather the sins of Athens. Thus, his irritation is righteous indignation, a byproduct of his new nature and his love for God when confronted with idol worship. But crucially, Paul does not take out his irritation on the Athenians. Instead, it's the proliferation of idols and outright sin in Athens that motivates him to share the truth of the gospel and God's *agape* love with the people.

However, most of the time, our touchiness and irritations are directed at human beings, not sin itself, and thus have nothing to do with *agape*. The hectic pace of our schedules, the pressure of deadlines, lack of sleep—and, yes, even anger—can lead us to be more quickly provoked. Others' sins and shortcomings can contribute to our irritated outbursts as well. Nonetheless, permitting our irritations to spill into our relationships with others, however briefly or rarely, is incompatible with the way of love to which God calls us.

Therefore, the real test of our spirituality is not what we do in the pew on a Sunday morning. It's what happens when we get home after church and when we're back at the office on Monday morning. It's how we conduct ourselves in the hallways at school and out on the athletic field. That's when the real "us" emerges for the world to see.

So, how do we react when our sibling scratches our brand-new car or leaks our private business at the supper table? Do we exchange sharp words? Do we lose our tempers with the ones we love?

Even when it seems like a necessary release or the only course of action, or when we're tempted to think it's for the other person's own good, we must be very cautious about giving someone else a piece of our mind. After all, most of us need all the mind God has given us. We need to be vigilant about giving it away. Yes, our temper may flare for an instant and then be back in check, but a bomb or grenade functions the same way—and look how much damage it does.

Giving others a piece of our mind leads to homes being filled with hurt and resentment instead of joy and peace. We need to stop inflicting our irritations on others and hurting the people we love most.

To this end, Christ-like love proves the best ointment for irritability. Love conquers tensions that make us uptight and angry. *Agape* is not irritable. It doesn't give into such temptations, but keeps its cool. It refuses to allow Satan room in our hearts to build a stronghold of sin. Instead, it stays in control of our words and actions—or rather, it leaves God in control.

Godly Accounting

...it [love] is not irritable or resentful... — **1 Corinthians 13:5**

Lastly, love is not **resentful**. 'Resentfulness' is an accounting term and has connotations of keeping a record of wrongs or offenses, as an accountant notes debts exactingly in his ledger. When we resent others, we bear a grudge against them because our minds have become little black books in which we record our every grievance.

A resentful disposition compels us to build cases against our family members, friends, colleagues, and fellow Christ-followers. As soon as someone does or says something we dislike, we begin observing and noting every misstep he or she makes. Then, at the most advantageous time, we open up our books to the person—often taking him or her by surprise—and demand a reckoning.

But such calculations aren't godly in the slightest. Our record of accounts proves nothing but our own pettiness and lack of love. Christ-like accounting does not record evil or store up resentment against those who may cross us.

Sadly, many people in the body of Christ seem unlikely ever to experience the liberation of God's accounting system. Paul faces a similar problem in his day—after all, he is writing his letter not to pagans, but to the church at Corinth. He finds himself compelled to instruct believers that they need to rid themselves of resentment and bitterness against each other. By the same token, we in the church today must take responsibility for our patterns of thinking about others.

After all, anyone can point out others' flaws. But only a godly man or woman, full of the love of Christ, can consistently look beyond other people's faults and see that they are made in the image of God. Love is always optimistic about other people, thinking the best of them and their potential in Christ. Love forgives.

By shedding resentment, we will find ourselves looking for ways to compliment, build up, and encourage one another, rather than tear one another down. Maintaining such an attitude, by God's grace, transforms our lives and the lives of the people around us.

Love's Code of Conduct

For he is like one who is inwardly calculating. "Eat and drink!" he says to you, but his heart is not with you. — **Proverbs 23:7**

The way of love, we have seen, trains us to think the best of others. To act like a Christian, we must first learn to think like a Christian, not *"like one who is inwardly calculating."* We must allow the truth of God's Word to run through our minds continuously. If we do so, then we'll find that God's truth and His love manifest consistently in our words and actions.

There is no other way to please the Lord. There is no other formula for practicing *agape*. Therefore, we must set our focus daily on the way of love to which God calls us. We must surrender the impulses of our human nature, our selfishness and pride, and give the Holy Spirit free rein in our lives.

Key to embracing love's code of conduct is realizing that the Spirit and His way of *agape* are not restrictive or binding, but liberating and energizing. Christ-like love fills us to overflowing with new life to replace our old ways of thinking. Then, instead of acting out of envy, arrogance, boastfulness, rudeness, selfishness, irritability, anger, and resentment, we will exude humility, kindness, consistency, politeness, selflessness, patience, and forgiveness.

May we praise God from the depths of our hearts for His abundant grace in offering us this *"more excellent way,"* in providing us the example of Christ, and in supplying the Holy Spirit to help us follow the path of His love. When we prayerfully cultivate the attitudes and characteristics of *agape* love in our heart, we can grow into the vibrant life He intends for us to enjoy!

Love's code of conduct is supernatural living at its best. As Christ-followers, we must allow our new nature as described in these verses to control us. In the created order, animals do instinctively what God created them to do. Fish do not attend classes to learn how to swim (even though they swim in pools). Birds don't attend flying school—they instinctively put out their wings and flap them in order to fly.

Because a fish has a fish's nature, it swims; because an eagle has an eagle's nature, it soars through the skies. Likewise, because we as Christ-followers have God's nature within us by the new birth, we love—because God's nature is alive within us!

When love's code of conduct is self-evident in our lives, we will be able to pray the prayer of St. Francis of Assisi:

Lord, make me an instrument of your peace:

where there is hatred, let me sow love;

where there is injury, pardon;

where there is doubt, faith;

where there is despair, hope;

where there is darkness, light;

and where there is sadness, joy.

O divine Master,

grant that I may not so much seek

to be consoled as to console,

to be understood as to understand,

to be loved as to love.

For it is in giving that we receive,

it is in pardoning that we are pardoned,

and it is in dying that we are born to eternal life.

Amen.[5]

WORKBOOK

Chapter 2 Questions

Question: What tends to trigger anger, impatience, and irritation in your life? What are some specific steps you can take, or habits you can develop, to ensure you meet and overcome these sources of agitation with God's love?

_____

_____

_____

_____

_____

_____

_____

_____

_____

_____

Question: When have you experienced kindness that changed the course of your day—or even your life? What are some specific ways you can show more kindness in your current relationships with family, friends, colleagues, neighbors, and members of your church?

_____
_____
_____
_____
_____
_____
_____
_____
_____
_____

Question: What was a time when you gave someone a piece of your mind? What was the result of your choice to let off steam in this way? What would have been a more loving way to handle the situation?

_____
_____
_____
_____
_____
_____
_____
_____
_____

Action: Surrender and crucify your old nature of envy, arrogance, boastfulness, rudeness, selfishness, irritability, anger, and resentment! Nail it to the cross every day, and instead choose to be patient, humble, kind, and forgiving in every circumstance. Let the love code of conduct govern your behavior regardless of where you are or with whom you're interacting. Train your mind on the Holy Spirit and allow God's *agape* love to fill your home, your church, and every one of your relationships!

Chapter 2 Notes

CHAPTER THREE

Love Has Heart

[Love] does not rejoice at wrongdoing, but rejoices with the truth. Love bears all things, believes all things, hopes all things, endures all things. — **1 Corinthians 13:6–7**

At the heart of Christ-like love is relentless courage that motivates and excites us to accomplish feats beyond anything we could ever have imagined. Courage isn't born in a crisis; it emerges from a crisis.

Craig Morton, quarterback of the Denver Broncos, led his team to their first Super Bowl appearance. Toward the end of the season, he was constantly injured, so after every game he had to have his knees packed in ice. He sometimes would be packed in ice for three or four hours, but he continued to play. Before getting to the AFC championship game, he spent three days in the hospital with his knees packed in ice.

When the Broncos played against the Oakland Raiders, he left the hospital and made his way to the chapel where they held their team prayer. He asked his coach if he could just go out for the coin toss and maybe play the first series of downs because he was hurting so badly.

Morton didn't participate in pre-game warm ups, but he participated in the coin toss and played the first series of downs. In fact, he stayed in the game until the very end. He ultimately passed for over 300 yards and three touchdowns. After the game, he was carried off the field to be packed in ice again.

That's what we call courage. And Christ-like love is courageous to the core. It's displayed in times of crisis and extreme challenge.

Christ-like love is relentless love. It is active love. It is not defensive. We've all known individuals who are defensive by nature. They have that defensive look about them. They watch their flank. They are forever on guard, unbelievingly cautious, always afraid that someone is going to get to them or rip them off. Again, this self-defensiveness melts away when Christ-like love is at the controls of our lives.

Standing for Truth

It does not rejoice at wrongdoing, but rejoices with the truth. **— 1 Corinthians 13:6**

Because love is courageous, it does not submit to momentary convenience. Rather, it stands for truth. *Agape* love *"does not rejoice in wrongdoing."* It does not delight in evil.

Unfortunately, ours is a generation of evil and terror. The media today thrives on scandal. It's known as "trash journalism." Newspapers, websites, and magazines are filled with descriptions of the most unspeakable acts that people commit against one another. When Christian leaders fall, or when those who claim the name of Jesus come up short, Satan especially rejoices. The Enemy celebrates the damage that comes to families and churches because of our failings.

When we are controlled by Christ-like love, we perceive the ways in which sin destroys our society and it breaks our hearts. When we read about disasters and destruction to human life, it saddens us. Instead of thinking that such things would never happen to us, or that those involved must have deserved what happened to them, we mourn and we pray.

We do not rejoice when evil comes upon others, regardless of what the rest of the world is doing. The world may feed off of the evil that befalls others, but God's people possess the courage to stand against wrongdoing, not rejoice in it.

As our society grows increasingly desensitized to sin and wickedness, the way of love insists that our hearts continue to break for others.

What does it do to us when we read of the growing drug addiction among our young people and the alcohol addiction among adults? Does it concern us when we read about students torturing homeless men and women to death? What goes through our minds when we read about young girls or women being raped in their homes?

Does it make any difference to us when a little child is kidnapped and killed? How do we react?

Paul says that love does not rejoice in these evil actions. Instead, love rejoices with the truth. Love and truth cannot be separated, for Jesus embodies both:

> *Jesus said to him, "I am the way, and the truth, and the life. No one comes to the Father except through me."* —
> **John 14:6**

We rejoice in the truth because Jesus Christ is *"the way, the truth, and the life."* He, in turn, rejoices to hear that His children are walking in truth. Because of Christ, we have the privilege of celebrating what is good, regardless of the situation, instead of wallowing in wickedness with the rest of the world.

The apostle John affirms: *"I have no greater joy than to hear that my children are walking in the truth"* (3 John 1:4). *Agape* love is possible because our hearts have been captured by truth. Christ's truth causes us to be full of rejoicing. The power of the living God has saved and transformed us!

Truth is strangely absent is our culture today. Several years ago, William Nagler came out with a book entitled *The Dirty Half Dozen: Six Radical Rules to Make Relationships Last.* The book was about the alternatives to second honeymoons and how couples could build romance into their lives. One of his rules was this (I'm not kidding): "Don't always tell the truth. Learn to lie. Truth requires total honesty. Total honesty requires infinite tact. Both are impossible. Neither exits. Lie a little."[6]

This is the philosophy that all too often is adapted by society at large, but Christ-like love runs counter to this mind-set. It never rejoices in wrongdoing!

Moreover, we rejoice in the fact that our name is recorded in heaven and this world is not our final home. Paul phrases it this way:

> *If in Christ we have hope in this life only, we are of all people most to be pitied.* — **1 Corinthians 15:19**

In other words, if we believe in Christ yet invest ourselves solely in the present life, we are in deep trouble. As Christ-followers, we have so much more to look forward to: a life together with Christ in heaven. Heaven is our true home, and if we aren't rejoicing in that fact, we're probably focused in the wrong direction.

Therefore, if we find ourselves preoccupied with evil—with unholy, sinful occurrences and practices that only pollute our hearts—we need to demonstrate holy, loving courage by turning away. Instead, let us turn toward Christ.

Wiping the Slate Clean

Love bears all things... — *1 Corinthians 13:7*

The word '*bears*' in this verse is a fascinating word. Literally, it means "to cover or to shelter." It suggests the idea of an umbrella that we put up, and into which we invite another person for shelter from the beating rain. Christ-like love acts as an umbrella and a roof over others, sheltering them and protecting them from the storms that sweep in upon them.

What happens when a brother or sister falls into sin? Do we lift them up or push them aside? Do we seek to provide shelter for them, or do we succumb to speaking unkindly about them?

What happens when we disagree with other Christ-followers or feel that other Christ-followers have wronged us? Do we go to them directly and seek to work out our personal differences, or do we gossip about them with our friends, building a case against them?

Gossip—unkind talk about others—is inconsistent with the *"more excellent way."*

Why do Christ-followers gossip? Perhaps speaking critically of others leads us to feel, at least briefly, that we are superior or that our own shortcomings are insignificant by comparison. Yet such behavior runs contrary to the truth, and thus to Jesus. It's a form of self-deception because we all fall short of His standard of love.

Furthermore, gossip is opposed to the truth because when we engage in gossip, we tend to treat the facts lightly. We speculate and hypothesize, allowing ourselves to fill in the gaps in our knowledge with the worst imaginable assumptions of others. Instead of pursuing the truth from reliable sources, we take the lazy way of inventing things that never happened so we can shoehorn people and events into a narrative that makes others look inferior.

When we are tempted to trade in gossip and criticism, we ought to remember that Jesus Christ died for each of us and has covered our faults in His blood, by love and grace. He has promised never again to bring them up. Christ-like love does not expose, but covers and protects:

As far as the east is from the west, so far does he remove our transgressions from us. — **Psalm 103:12**

You will cast all our sins into the depths of the sea. —**Micah 7:19**

I will forgive their iniquity, and I will remember there sin no more. — **Jeremiah 31:34**

Thus, when we confess our sins, God wipes the slate clean. And if He doesn't talk about our sins, then we ought not to be talking about one another's failings. Others' sins should break our hearts. Therefore, we should pray and do everything in our power as Christ-followers to reach out to those who are persisting in sin and help them back into a fully loving relationship with Christ.

The Benefit of the Doubt

Love bears all things, believes all things, hopes all things, endures all things. — **1 Corinthians 13:7**

Moreover, love requires us to maintain faith, belief, and hope courageously, regardless of circumstances. Love gives the benefit of the doubt under every situation, even when it would be easier or more convenient to gossip, cast doubt, hide behind suspicions, or otherwise assume the worst.

In saying that love "*believes all things*," Paul does not claim that love is gullible, unreasonable, or naïve. Rather, he means that Christ-followers do not engage in suspicious dispositions. We learn to accept people and circumstances at face value. When we communicate with other people, instead of assuming the worst to reinforce our prejudices, we remove our filters of suspicion and refrain from casting judgment. We start listening for what other people are truly saying.

Christ-like love believes. It trusts confidently in God and His Word, understanding that behind every circumstance of life stands a sovereign God. True Christ-followers don't waste time questioning Him, doubting each other, or fighting and fretting over aspects of life that only He can control.

What a tremendous quality this is. How great to be liberated from always suspecting the worst in others! All too many of us live our lives without trusting anyone or anything. We have misgivings about the government, the store clerk, our neighbors, and our friends. Parents are suspicious of their children, and children are suspicious of their parents.

When we are controlled by suspicion, we're miserable. We simply exist through life. We withdraw and become islands of loneliness and discontent.

Christ-like love is not suspicious. It *"believes"* and understands that behind all that happens to a Christ-follower stands a sovereign God who has everything under control. This unique kind of love recognizes that God has a purpose in everything He allows to come to pass. Setbacks do not cause us to doubt God or question His will for us. We simply rest in His all-encompassing love.

In summary, Christ-like love is the "attitude indicator" of the heart. Aviation experts tell us that the attitude of an airplane is the position of the airplane to the horizon. When an airplane is climbing, it's in a nose-high attitude. When a plane is descending, it's in the nose-down attitude. Pilots are greatly concerned about the attitude of an airplane because the attitude determines the altitude. A nose-high attitude is necessary for flying; a nose-down attitude, if not corrected, results in a crash.

Love at its core rejoices, protects, and trusts. These attitudes keep us in a nose-high position so that our spiritual lives do not crash. These are the inner graces that give us the energy to be patient and kind, not envious, arrogant and rude!

Enduring Love

Love ... endures all things. — *1 Corinthians 13:7*

The word 'endures' means "to remain under" and paints the picture of bearing up under a heavy load.[7] Christ-like love can take the pressure! It's steadfast and sure because it is anchored to Christ, the Solid Rock.

Christ-like love endures the blessings of life as well as the burdens. Christ-like love survives the tests as well as the triumphs. Christ-like love doesn't fluctuate with the circumstances of life that change constantly. It holds its ground: it bears up under difficult situations, and it knows how to keep going when others have given up.

This, again, is a quality that all Christ-followers must seek to cultivate. Just as a long-distance runner develops endurance through disciplining his body for the race by getting up early in the morning and running miles while the rest of the world sleeps, so Christ-followers must develop endurance through Bible study and prayer.

Anyone can rejoice in times of great blessing, but it is during times when God seems far away, strangely silent and unresponsive to our prayers, that we are too easily tempted to give up and ignore the spiritual disciples that build endurance. How tragic!

We need the counsel of Christ, who explains in John 16:33, *"In the world you will have tribulation. But take heart; I have overcome the world."* And again, the apostle John affirms that *"he who is in you is greater than he who is in the world"* (1 John 4:4).

Trials come to all of us. But as we endure in the strength of Christ, these trials become golden opportunities for God to display His power and awesome love.

The reward for this kind of endurance is great. James tells us: *"Blessed is the man who remains steadfast under trial, for when he has stood the test he will receive the crown of life, which God has promised to those who love him"* (James 1:12). Though problems may beat us down, enduring love enables us to get up and never be counted out!

WORKBOOK

Chapter 3 Questions

Question: How should you respond when friends or family members gossip? How can you resist the temptation to participate in gossip?

_____

_____

_____

_____

_____

_____

_____

_____

_____

_____

_____

Question: Whom do you need to start giving the benefit of the doubt, and how can you demonstrate this today?

_____

_____

_____

_____

_____

_____

_____

_____

_____

_____

Question: What are some disciplines or daily habits that will help strengthen the endurance of your Christ-like love?

_____

_____

_____

_____

_____

_____

_____

_____

_____

_____

Action: Live courageously in Christ's love, standing up for the way of _agape_ and not delighting in gossip or evil of any kind. Endure all trials and obstacles that come your way, taking heart in the knowledge that Christ is greater than the Enemy. Overcome wickedness with love in every part of your life!

Chapter 3 Notes

_____

_____

_____

_____

_____

_____

_____

_____

_____

_____

_____

_____

_____

_____

_____

_____

_____

_____

_____

_____

_____

_____

_____

CHAPTER FOUR

Love Has Spirit

When we hear the word 'spirit,' what comes to mind? We might recall high school pep rallies, when the students would show up in their school colors and work themselves into an enthusiastic frenzy in preparation for taking on a rival school.

Or we might reflect on the spirit of ingenuity and creativity that motivates so many entrepreneurs and scientists in the world today. We are living in a generation for which technological and medical advances are exploding beyond measure.

Look no further than the smartphone: with a device that fits in our pocket, we can send and receive mail, draft documents, conduct research, purchase anything from groceries to a new car, manage bank accounts, talk face-to-face with a family member, and hold business conferences. A can-do spirit of progress infects and influences wide swathes of our economy, political culture, and scientific pursuits.

Christ-like love not only possesses a courageous heart, but it also has a contagious spirit. If our lives as Christians do not inspire others to want what we have, or if they don't notice any difference at all in us, then we are not walking the way of love. We are children of King Jesus, who calls us to infect others with His love. Paul describes this spirit articulately.

Love Hopes

*Love ... hopes all things... — **1 Corinthians 13:7***

Christ-like love *"hopes."* Jesus' love is optimistic. Whereas optimism sees the possibilities in spite of the problems, pessimism is overwhelmed with difficulties. Love's antidote for pessimism is hope. Rather than looking for the reasons why something cannot be accomplished, we must *"hope all things"* and look to God because He is in control. Our optimism stems from the fact that our focus is Christ. We don't have to know all the answers, because we know the One who does.

When we are optimists led by God's love, we are always looking for the best, including the best ways to advance the kingdom of God. Christ's presence in our lives empowers us with a sense of hope and optimism that helps us to rise above our circumstances.

One summer when I was in seminary, I had the opportunity to work for Johnson Outboard Marine Corporation. I was about twenty-two or twenty-three years old at the time, and I remember a bunch of the older guys making remarks like, "Boy, John. I am glad I am not as young as you are. Oh my, all the problems you are going to have to deal with." I suspect these pessimistic comments derived from their frustration with their own lives. But I remained optimistic about my future because I had hope in Jesus.

I'm reminded of David, the Psalmist who faced all kinds of difficulties and problems. King Saul tries to kill him and David has to flee for his life. His own son rebels against him and seeks to take the throne from him. Yet David remains optimistic. In Psalm 34:1 he exclaims, "*I will bless the LORD at all time; his praise shall continually be in my mouth.*" Wow—that is hope!

Our optimism need not be blind, but we do need to focus more on our vertical relationship with the King of kings and Lord of lords than we do on our horizontal, earthly existence. We must look ahead to the incredible things God has planned for us in building His kingdom, instead of forever staring into the rearview mirror.

When we gaze into the mirror, we cannot help but catch a glimpse of ourselves, and our personal limitations circumscribe our dreams. But when a contagious spirit of optimism directs our eyes to the way of love that lies ahead, we find ourselves focusing on God—and He enables us to envision and achieve dreams far beyond the ordinary.

Love Never Ends

Love never ends. — *1 Corinthians 13:8*

Paul brings this section to a close by saying, "*Love never ends.*" Christ-like love never fails or loses its position. The ancient Greeks used to say, "Nothing will last." Paul explains, in direct contrast, "Love never ends."

The word "*ends*" here has two distinct meanings. In classical Greek, it paints the picture of a bad actor or a villain being hissed off the stage.[8] Authentic Christ-like love is never hissed off the stage of life. It lives now and will continue to live throughout all eternity.

The second word-picture of "*ends*" is that of a fading flower with falling petals.[9] But again, Christ-like love does not fade, wither, or fall away. Indeed, as Paul continues, he declares that Christ-like love outlasts the God-given spiritual gifts, which the Corinthians have been over-emphasizing, misusing, and even abusing. We must not forget that 1 Corinthians 13 is sandwiched in between chapters 12 and 14 so we will understand that Christ-like love is to characterize our lives more than any exercise of any spiritual gift we have received from God.

Indeed, love is the capstone of the fruit of the Spirit, as Paul underscores in Galatians 6:22: "*The fruit of the Spirit is love.*" Christ-like love brings "*joy, peace, patience, kindness, goodness, faithfulness, gentleness and self-control*" into our lives (Galatians 6:22–23).

God is much more interested in our character than He is in the way we carry out and employ the spiritual gifts

He gives us. Though spiritual gifts are the means of great blessing and edification, they are not eternal. Christ-like love outlasts them all!

The gift of prophecy passes away, according to Paul: *"As for prophecies, they will pass away"* (1 Corinthians 13:8b). The gift of prophecy is a marvelous gift. To be able to take the Word of God and cause it to shine in the hearts of people so that they will understand the "good news" of the gospel is a wondrous and incredible gift.

But someday, when we stand before God, there will be no need for the prophet because God Himself will be our teacher and we'll spend hours at the feet of Jesus, learning from Him.

The gift of tongues will cease as well. Paul says, *"As for tongues, they will cease"* (1 Corinthians 13:8b). This gift, which the Corinthians mistakenly believe is superior to all of the other gifts, also has no eternal significance. Why spend so much time arguing and hassling over a spiritual gift that has no eternal value?

The same is true for the gift of knowledge, of which he writes: *"...as for knowledge, it will pass away."* (1 Corinthians 13:8c). This wondrous gift, the ability to see things from God's point of view, also vanishes.

Christ-like love, to the contrary, lasts. It never ends. Love is greater than any spiritual gift, and the jealousy over spiritual gifts that divides the Corinthian church is not healthy. This is why Paul boldly declares, "Love is the greatest!"

In brief, love outlasts anything that is earthly. All of the great buildings man has constructed and all of the great art collections that man has accumulated one day will crumble and fall. Look at what has happened to the Hanging Gardens of Babylon, the majestic temples of Greece and Rome, and the great museums in Europe. Castles and architectural masterpieces, in all of their opulence, don't last. When all else fails, Christ-like love never ends!

WORKBOOK

Chapter 4 Questions

Question: Why is Christ-like love optimistic instead of pessimistic? In which areas of your life has pessimism taken root? How can God's love help you replace pessimism with optimism?

_____

_____

_____

_____

_____

_____

_____

_____

_____

_____

_____

_____

Question: What aspects of Christian character pose a particular challenge to you? How is this characteristic a fruit of Christ-like love? What is one specific way you can cultivate it?

_____

_____

_____

_____

_____

_____

_____

_____

_____

_____

Question: What are some other specific examples of contagiously Christ-like habits you can practice to spread the hopefulness and joy of _agape_ love?

_____

_____

_____

_____

_____

_____

_____

_____

_____

_____

Action: Be optimistic in your expressions of love: act and speak and think in such a way that God's transforming love spreads contagiously from you to the heart of every person with whom you come into contact!

Chapter 4 Notes

CHAPTER FIVE

Love Has Staying Power

For we know in part and we prophecy in part, but when the perfect comes, the partial will pass away. When I was a child, I spoke like a child, I thought like a child, I reasoned like a child. When I became a man, I gave up childish ways. For now we see in a mirror dimly, but then face to face. Now I know in part; then I shall know fully, even as I have been fully known. — 1 Corinthians 13:9–12

We live in a disposable world in which nothing lasts. Even as human beings, we are born to die. Manufactures create products designed to fail because they wear out. Years ago, we would buy an appliance and it would last thirty or forty years. I remember buying a refrigerator and freezer and expecting both to function for decades.

These days, we are doing well if we get five years before an appliance starts leaking, falling apart, or ruining everything we put in it. Then, of course, the appliance store is perfectly happy to sell us a replacement that's newer, shinier, more environmentally friendly, and equally short-lived.

We buy a new car or a new home and before we know it, there is constant repair and upkeep. The smell of newness wears off, rust sets in, and paint fades.

The last time we went to the doctor, we thought it would be our last visit. But we've been back several times since. No matter how healthy or strong we feel right now, our muscles will give out one day. No matter how much we exercise, someday our faces will wrinkle and our stomachs will sag.

But God's love has staying power. It hangs tough. It doesn't give up or let us down, because it is locked into an unfailing Christ.

Paul intends his letter to the Christ-followers at Corinth to be a wake-up call. They need to get their priorities straight because wrong priorities are creating strife in the body of Christ and leading them into sin. Love is not prevailing in the Corinthian church at this time, but love is all they ultimately need.

Incidentally, "Love Is All You Need" is a line from one of the Beatles' popular songs. At the height of Beatlemania, back in the Sixties, the band claimed to be more popular than Jesus. Five decades later, their band is long dissolved and half of the members are no longer living. But Jesus Christ, the King of kings and Lord of lords, is still King!

When we are loving God and loving each other, we are preparing for eternity. The rest is just details.

Partial Made Perfect

For we know in part and we prophesy in part... — 1 Co-rinthians 13:9

Earthly knowledge, at best, is partial. Even those who have been given a special gift by God to understand and assimilate knowledge only *"know in part."* Man's knowledge is always incomplete. No one knows all there is to know. In fact, the longer we go to school, the more we realize how much we do not know!

Paul continues by saying *"we prophecy in part."* Though God does not reveal everything to His servants, as we study His Word, we are given brief glimpses of truth, which we can cause to shine in the hearts of others, in turn. No prophet has been given all the revelations of God. That's why the more we read the Bible, the more precious and revealing it becomes. We find ourselves saying: "Wow, *that's* in God's Word!"

However, the day will come when everything that is partial or incomplete will be made perfect, according to Paul. This is a reference to the second coming of Christ, when the heavenly kingdom of God will arrive on earth. In the future, we will clearly perceive perfection as God reveals it to us in person:

...but when the perfect comes, the partial will pass away. — 1 Corinthians 13:10

Paul doesn't say gifts of the Spirit are not useful, but rather he counsels us that they are partial at best. Therefore, these gifts are inferior to Christ-like love, which is eternal and permanent.

Then, too, Paul tells the Corinthians pointedly, there is no sense squabbling over which spiritual gifts are superior to others: such gifts are only partial, not perfect. When Christ returns, the gifts God grants us to minister to each other in the here and now will become irrelevant—superseded by the brilliant reality of God's eternal kingdom.

Our Childish Ways

Paul employs two illustrations to help the Corinthians understand the temporary nature of the spiritual gifts, in contrast to *agape* love. First, he provides them the metaphor of a child, in contrast to a mature adult:

> When I was a child, I spoke like a child, I thought like a child, I reasoned like a child. When I became a man, I gave up childish ways. — *1 Corinthians 13:11*

A child thinks, reasons, and evaluates differently than an adult does. Things that occupy a child's mind—toys, for instance—are not things that occupy most adults' minds. What is important to a child may be incidental to an adult.

Likewise, the same is true in heaven. Most of the interests, passions, and priorities that motivated us during our earthly lives will pass into oblivion, or seem unimportant and irrelevant. They will fade away as soon as we directly experience the radiance of God's personal presence.

Moreover, the troubles we endure down here won't matter much when Jesus ushers us into perfection. We will suddenly realize how much energy we wasted on non-essentials, majoring on minors and specializing in trivia, rather than living the life of Christ-like love toward God and our fellow man. Paul's point is clear: Grow up—become adults and learn to love!

Second, Paul uses the metaphor of a mirror to explain the incompleteness of the lesser spiritual gifts:

> *For now we see in a mirror dimly, but then face to face. Now I know in part; then I shall know fully, even as I have been fully known.* — **1 Corinthians 13:12**

The word *"dimly"* here refers to a mirror of polished metal.[10] Mirrors in ancient Corinth were not of the greatest quality, and the reflections that they would produce often were distorted. By looking in a mirror, the Corinthians could only see with partial accuracy.

We don't fully understand everything that God does, from His deep mysteries to His everyday interactions with us. Why hasn't God made all of this clear? Because we are seeing *"in a mirror dimly."*

There is much in this world we don't understand because we only have partial knowledge. We see life in riddles. We're puzzled about many things. The focus of life is not clear; there is a lot of fuzz around the edges.

We don't understand why we must endure trials and hardships. We don't understand why there is evil in the world and why God doesn't do something about it. We're bothered because God doesn't answer our prayers and seems oblivious to the many injustices in our world. We don't grasp the deep mysteries of God like the Trinity or the exact sequence of end-time events.

There is so much that is an enigma to us. Why? We only have partial knowledge.

John explains our partial understanding thusly:

> See what kind of love the Father has given to us, that we should be called children of God; and so we are. The reason why the world does not know us is that it did not know him. Beloved, we are God's children now, and what we will be has not yet appeared; but we know that when he appears we shall be like him, because we shall see him as he is. And everyone who thus hopes in him purifies himself as he is pure. — *1 John 3:1–3*

We are God's children, but what we will become hasn't yet come to pass. We know that when He appears, we shall be like Him, but the details are not yet clear to us. We shall see Him face to face when we are in His presence, but we don't yet know how He will appear to us.

When these events transpire, however, the things that once baffled and puzzled us will do so no longer. The human limitations we experience now will all be a thing of the past. The things we wrestled with will no longer occupy our minds—for we will be with Him.

Paul's counsel to us is simply to concentrate on the coming perfection, not upon the peripheral knowledge that we may possess right now. One day our limited capacities and our physical limitations will be expanded so that we resemble Jesus, whose company we can then enjoy forever. Our thoughts, goals, and agendas must become subject to that future moment when we see Him face to face.

Therefore, let's live every day with Christ at the center of our hearts and minds—because Christ and His love will never end!

WORKBOOK

Chapter 5 Questions

Question: What are some things, or aspects of life on earth, to which you're attached but which you know you won't be able to take to heaven with you?

_____

_____

_____

_____

_____

_____

_____

_____

_____

_____

_____

Question: How do you prepare for eternity in the way you spend your time, energy, and resources? How exactly could you grow in your stewardship of God's blessings?

_____

_____

_____

_____

_____

_____

_____

_____

_____

_____

Question: What is the single most import step or significant change you need to make in your life, beginning today, to ensure that you maintain a Christ-centered life?

_____

_____

_____

_____

_____

_____

_____

_____

_____

_____

Action: Devote yourself to Christ in all that you do! In every decision about how to run your life, where to concentrate your energy, and how to manage the resources and gifts with which God has blessed you, be a mature follower of Christ—who understands that some things are temporary but only Christ and His love are eternal. Be deliberate in your love for God and others, and invest in *agape* so that it's continually growing in every area of your life.

Chapter 5 Notes

_____

_____

_____

_____

_____

_____

_____

_____

_____

_____

_____

_____

_____

_____

_____

_____

_____

_____

_____

_____

_____

_____

CONCLUSION

Pursue Love

So now faith, hope, and love, abide, these three; but the greatest of these is love. — **1 Corinthians 13:13**

Paul's conclusion is climactic. Faith, hope, and love are virtues that abide forever. They continue throughout all eternity and we, as Christ-followers need to pursue all of them.

Faith, we recall, is a dominant theme in Paul's life. It is central to his teaching and living. For example, in his letter to the Galatians, Paul exclaims, "*I have been crucified with Christ. It is no longer I who live, but Christ who lives in me. And the life I now live in the flesh I live by faith in the Son of God who loved me and gave himself for me.*" Yet *agape* love supersedes faith.

Hope is another virtue that captures Paul's heart. He speaks repeatedly about the hope we as Christ-followers have because of the resurrection of Jesus Christ from the grave. In 1 Corinthians 15:14–17 he writes:

And if Christ has not been raised, then our preaching is in vain and your faith is in vain. We are even found to be misrepresenting God, because we testified about God that he raised Christ, whom he did not raise if it is true that the dead are not raised. For if the dead are not raised, not even Christ has been raised. And if Christ has not been raised, your faith is futile and you are still in your sins.

If this life were all there is, we would be hopeless and have no certainty of heaven. But because Christ conquered death in resurrection and remains in a risen state, eternal life is not a figment of our imagination—rather, it is a glorious hope!

But the greatest virtue of all is love. ***Agape* love is the greatest because God is its source.** God cannot exercise faith or cherish hope. The Bible declares, on the other hand, that God not only possesses love but also *is* love.

The apostle John testifies in 1 John 4:7–8: *"Beloved, let us love one another, for love is from God, and whoever loves has been born of God and knows God. Anyone who does not love does not know God, because God is love."*

***Agape* love is the greatest because Christ is its supreme manifestation.** Christ expresses the love of God to man in laying down His life upon the cross for the sins of the whole world. Jesus says in John 15:13, *"Greater love has no one than this, that someone lay down his life for his friends."* Christ's sacrificial death on the cross makes visible to us the great love He has for each one of us.

***Agape* love is the greatest because it is central to the teachings of Christ.** In His great Sermon on the

Mount, Jesus teaches, "*You have heard that it was said, 'You shall love your neighbor and hate your enemy.' But I say to you, Love your enemies and pray for those who persecute you...*" (Matthew 5:43–44). In the Upper Room with His disciples, just before going to the cross, Jesus explains the unique feature of this kind of other-centered, divine love:

> *A new commandment I give to you, that you love one another: just as I have loved you, you also are to love one another. By this all people will know that you are my disciples if you have love for one another.* — **John 13:34–35**

As followers of Christ, we know that *agape* love is the greatest; it is the badge of our discipleship!

Back in the day, I played a little high school football. I liked to play defensive end. The one thing I especially enjoyed doing was going after the quarterback. If I could catch and tackle him from his blind side, chances were that he would fumble the ball. That was a thrill—to pursue him, run him down, and knock that ball out of his hands. What a rush!

That's the sense of the word 'pursue.' As Christ-followers, Paul calls us to make love our first pursuit:

> *Pursue love, and earnestly desire the spiritual gifts.* — **1 Corinthians 14:1**

Love of God, and love for one another, must be our primary goals in life. We must intentionally and swiftly run after love, and then we must allow it to consume us. There is immense spiritual value in both the pursuit and the final victory.

Of all the chief gifts of God—faith, hope, and love— love is the greatest, as Paul writes in 1 Corinthians 13:13. Each of these gifts is to be held fast and nurtured, as are the miraculous spiritual gifts in which the Corinthians are putting great stock. Yet, of the three supreme gifts of God, love rises high above the rest.

In the very next chapter, 1 Corinthians 14:1, Paul continues by commanding us to *"pursue love"* each day, in every aspect of our lives and relationships. We must pursue the way of love vigorously, as if we were a defensive end rushing the quarterback!

The word 'pursue' here is the same word that Paul uses in his first letter to Timothy:

> But as for you, O man of God, flee these things. Pursue righteousness, godliness, faith, love, steadfastness, gentleness. — *1 Timothy 6:11*

'Pursue' is an active word implying strenuous effort and unqualified concentration. Christ-followers are exhorted to run after love with the same abandon that a football defensive end pursues the quarterback on the opposing team.

To experience and cultivate Christ-like *agape* love, we must first receive Jesus as our personal Savior. There is no way on God's green earth that any one of us can practice the way of love without Jesus in our life. Personally embracing Him and His loving self-sacrifice on the cross requires an act of faith on our part. In return, we receive the Holy Spirit into our heart. Then the Holy Spirit pours *agape* into our life:

> *Hope does not put us to shame, because God's love has been poured into our hearts through the Holy Spirit who has been given to us.* — **Romans 5:5**

As His love pours in, we empty ourselves of sin and the other junk of life. Then, when we're full of the Spirit, we will find ourselves unable to remain at odds with others. Indeed, we become the dwelling place of God Himself: *"Do you not know that you are God's temple and that God's Spirit dwells (lives) in you?"* (1 Corinthians 3:16).

Thus, Paul encourages the Philippians:

> *And it is my prayer that your love may abound more and more, with knowledge and all discernment.* — **Philippians 1:9**

The word 'abound' means to overflow continually. Therefore, we allow God's love to overflow in our hearts, like floodwaters overflowing the dam of our old nature!

When we live and love by faith, we are telling Jesus: "Lord, by faith, I am going to love You more today than I did yesterday. By faith I am going to extend love to my family and my church family. I will love my neighbors and co-workers. And I will love by faith, not by the emotions and attitudes of my natural self.

"By God's grace, I will be other-centered rather than self-centered. No more spiritual mediocrity for me. I will give of myself rather than expecting others to give. In every corner of my heart and my life, I am adopting the *more excellent way*—the way of love."

The story is told of a Rhodes scholar who once wrote a paper on the theme "What is love?" His research was extensive. He read and reviewed hundreds of books. He spent several months analyzing and organizing his research. When he was ready to present his work to his publisher, arrangements were made with a stenographer to type the manuscript.

When he walked into her office for the very first time, something electric happened. Their eyes met; their pulses quickened. Love at first sight swept them off their feet. The Rhodes scholar discovered that what he'd been writing about was not merely a theory to be explored, but a reality he could personally experience and enjoy.

For *agape* love to be released in our lives, we need a personal encounter with Christ. Once our eyes meet His at the foot of the cross, we will experience the power of His presence and the magnitude of His love. We will never be the same again.

First Corinthians 13 is God's blueprint for a beautiful life. It can be yours today!

Notes

1. Vine, W. E. "Colossians 3:14: Charity." *W. E. Vine's New Testament Word Pictures: Romans to Revelation.* Thomas Nelson, 2015, p. 589.
2. Sweeting, George. "Love Minus Love Equals Nothing." *Moody Church Media.* Moody Church Media Ministry, 1965. https://www.moodymedia.org/articles/love-minus-love-equals-nothing/
3. Allen, Charles Livingstone. *The Miracle of Love.* F. H. Revell, 1972.
4. Handford, Thomas W. *Two Thousand and Ten Choice Quotations in Poetry and Prose.* Belford-Clarke, 1890. p. 348.
5. "Peace Prayer of Saint Francis." *Loyola Press.* 2017. https://www.loyolapress.com/our-catholic-faith/prayer/traditional-catholic-prayers/saints-prayers/peace-prayer-of-saint-francis

6. Nagler, William. *The Dirty Half Dozen: Six Radical Rules to Make Relationships Last.* Grand Central Publishing, 1992.
7. "5278. hupomenó." *Bible Hub.* From *HELPS Word-studies*, HELPS Ministries, Inc., 1987, 2011. http://biblehub.com/greek/5278.htm
8. Sweeting, George. *Love Is the Greatest.* Moody Press, 1974, p. 95.
9. Ibid.
10. "1 Corinthians 13:12." *Bible Hub.* From Albert Barnes, *Barnes' Notes on the Bible*, 1834, in Internet Sacred Texts Archives. http://biblehub.com/commentaries/1_corinthians/13-12.htm

About the Author

JOHN R. STRUBHAR, D.MIN.

Dr. John Strubhar was born in Chicago, Illinois, and attended Westmont College for one year before graduating with a B.A. from Summit Christian College in 1969. He continued his theological studies at Trinity Evangelical Divinity School in Deerfield, Illinois, receiving a M.Div. in 1973; a Th.M. in homiletics and pastoral theology in 1975; and a D.Min. in Church Administration and Revitalization in 1980.

Currently, Dr. Strubhar is serving as an Interim Pastor with **Interim Pastor Ministries** (IPM). Prior to this ministry, he was the Lead Pastor at Maywood Evangelical Free Church in Rockford, IL. His previous ministries involved serving as the Executive Pastor at the Boca Raton Community Church, Boca Raton, FL; Superintendent for the Great Lakes District of the Evangelical Free Church of America; and Lead Pastor of churches in Indiana, Illinois, and California. He is ordained by the Evangelical Free Church of America and is a lifetime member of the EFCA Ministerial Association.

In addition to his pastoral duties, Dr. Strubhar has served as a graduate assistant and guest lecturer at Trinity Evangelical Divinity School, Summit Christian College, and Moody Bible Institute (*Correspondence Department*). He has also ministered as a church consultant and conference speaker. He has been a Director on the Board of Governors at Summit Christian College, the Pastor's Advisory Council at Trinity College, the American Board of Missions to the Jews, the Board of Directors for the Evangelical Free Church of America, and Reaching Indians Ministries International.

Dr. Strubhar co-authored a book with the late Dr. Lloyd Perry entitled ***Evangelistic Preaching: A Step by Step Guide to Pulpit Evangelism***, published by Moody Press in 1979 and reprinted by Wipf and Stock Publishers in 2000. He has also contributed several chapters to two men's devotional books: ***Time Out***, published by Evergreen in 1989, and ***Take Five***, published by Broadman and Holman in 1994.

Dr. Strubhar and his wife Sandy reside in Buckeye, Arizona. They have three grown children and eleven grandchildren.

About Sermon To Book

SermonToBook.com began with a simple belief: that sermons should be touching lives, *not* collecting dust. That's why we turn sermons into high-quality books that are accessible to people all over the globe.

Turning your sermon series into a book exposes more people to God's Word, better equips you for counseling, accelerates future sermon prep, adds credibility to your ministry, and even helps make ends meet during tight times.

John 21:25 tells us that the world itself couldn't contain the books that would be written about the work of Jesus Christ. Our mission is to try anyway. Because in heaven, there will no longer be a need for sermons or books. Our time is now.

If God so leads you, we'd love to work with you on your sermon or sermon series.

Visit www.sermontobook.com to learn more.

www.ingramcontent.com/pod-product-compliance
Lightning Source LLC
Chambersburg PA
CBHW060210070426

42447CB00035B/2921